Mythical Beasts
MONSTERS
OF THE
GODS

Thanks to the creative team:
Senior Editor: Matthew Rake
Designer: Lauren Woods and collaborate agency

Original edition copyright 2015 by Hungry Tomato Ltd.

Copyright © 2016 by Lerner Publishing Group, Inc.

Hungry Tomato™ is a trademark of Lerner Publishing Group, Inc.

Hungry Tomato™
A division of Lerner Publishing Group, Inc.
241 First Avenue North
Minneapolis, MN 55401 USA

For reading levels and more information, look up this title at www.lernerbooks.com.

Main body text set in Galahad Std 12/1.5
Typeface provided by Adobe Systems.

Library of Congress Cataloging-in-Publication Data

Peebles, Alice.
    Monsters of the gods / by Alice Peebles ; illustrated by Nigel Chilvers.
    pages cm. — (Mythical beasts)
        ISBN 978-1-4677-6342-4 (lb : alk. paper —
    ISBN 978-1-4677-7654-7 (pb : alk. paper) —
    ISBN 978-1-4677-7218-1 (eb pdf)
        1. Gods, Roman—Juvenile literature. 2. Mythology, Roman—Juvenile literature. I. Chilvers, Nigel, illustrator. II. Title.
    BL803.P44 2016
    398'.469—dc23   2015001594

Manufactured in the United States of America
1 – VP – 7/15/15

Mythical Beasts

MONSTERS
OF THE
GODS

By Alice Peebles

Illustrated by Nigel Chilvers

HUNGRY TOMATO™

Minneapolis

"With a deep roar, the water swirled downward, sucked by a force that tore the ocean wide open, right down to the dark seabed. The boats slipped helplessly into the vortex . . ."

Contents

Monsters of the Gods

Meet the ten most fearsome monsters from mythology, created, nurtured and used by the gods to wreak havoc in the human world . . .

Here you will find the notorious Minotaur that fed on living flesh and the remorseless guardian-beasts of the ancient underworlds, Cerberus and Ammut, who terrorized spirits after death. Some, like the Gorgon Medusa and the nine-headed Hydra, are themselves the offspring of monsters . . . so no wonder they have unique powers and grotesque qualities, such as many heads. Others are strange fusions of human and animal or several animals together.

Not only on and under the earth, but in the ocean depths, too, humans are not safe. That terrible duo, Scylla and Charybdis, prey on unsuspecting sailors by plucking them from their ships or dragging them to a watery grave. But which of all these is the most ferocious of all? You're about to find out.

Each of the ten beasts is shown in a vivid scene inspired by tales handed down since ancient times. You can read about where each story comes from and turn to the back to find out more.

The beasts appear in ranked order from least powerful to most powerful, and they are given scores from 1 to 10 for each of five categories: Strength, Repulsiveness, Special Powers, Ferocity, and Invincibility. You'll also find a suggestion on how to defeat or neutralize each one. You can also think up your own methods, but some creatures seem so invincible . . .

Are you ready to face the vicious, slime-spreading Harpies or trail through the African jungle to meet the elephant-snake Grootslang? They're waiting for you . . .

Winged Avengers
The Harpies

"No one reveals the secrets of the gods!" thundered Zeus. "Punish this mortal!" he ordered the vulture women, pointing down to Earth, at a tiny dot that was the palace of King Phineus.

The Harpies' great wings carried them faster than storm winds to the banquet hall of Phineus. They overturned tables, covered food in filthy slime and pursued Phineus, stabbing at his eyes.

"You shall never eat in peace again!" they shrieked as he tried to defend himself. And from then on, whenever he raised a morsel to his mouth, the Harpies snatched the food away, leaving him hungry and desperate.

How to defeat the Harpies

Powerful allies are needed to fend them off. Phineus was only freed of them when Jason and the Argonauts visited him. Two of the Argonauts were the winged sons of the North Wind, and they chased away the Harpies.

Where does this myth come from?

The Greek poets Homer and Hesiod imagined the Harpies as fair creatures that flew faster than any wind or bird. Other Greek and Roman writers depicted them as ugly winged monsters, who snatched people from Earth or persecuted them for misdeeds on behalf of the gods.

Beast Power

Strength
2

Repulsiveness
5

Special Powers
3

Ferocity
6

Invincibility
4

Total
20/50

The Bull of Heaven
Gugalanna

Gugalanna, the mighty bull who was also a god, was wreaking havoc in the kingdom of Gilgamesh. He drank up all its rivers and stripped its palm trees of dates, its orchards of oranges, and its fields of grass.

Grabbing his spear, Gilgamesh stormed off to meet Gugalanna on the land he had blasted. As the bull came thundering toward him in a cloud of dust, Gilgamesh leaped to one side and drove his spear more than halfway into the beast's neck.

With a mighty jerk, Gugalanna reared up and toppled over. As he landed, his head was completely torn off. Great was the joy of Gilgamesh and his people.

How to defeat Gugalanna

A less powerful and well-armed person than Gilgamesh could perhaps neutralize Gugalanna's great strength by appealing to his sweet tooth and feeding him honey cakes containing a sleeping drug.

Where does this myth come from?

The story is part of the earliest work of literature, the Epic of Gilgamesh. *It originated in Mesopotamia, roughly the area of modern Iraq, and the most complete version was written on tablets around 1200 BCE. Gilgamesh is believed to have ruled the city of Uruk around 2600 BCE.*

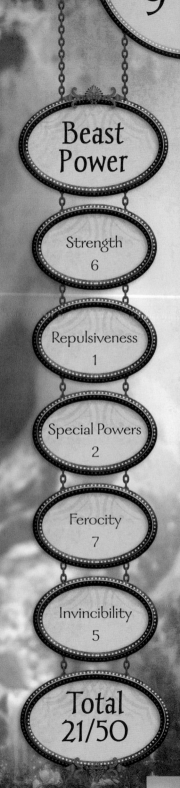

Beast Power

Strength
6

Repulsiveness
1

Special Powers
2

Ferocity
7

Invincibility
5

Total
21/50

Snake-Haired Beasts
The Gorgons

"Come, sisters, see what we have here!"
Medusa called her two Gorgon sisters
from their cave on the edge of the ocean.
Her words were just so many snarls
and hisses to the young man who had
ventured too far from home.

At once the lad tried to turn and run,
but somehow, as if in a dream, he could not
move a limb. He stared up at the huge, scaled
body, the hands of bronze, the snakes that
writhed around Medusa's loathsome face, as
he gradually turned to stone . . .

How to defeat the Gorgons

Looking on Medusa's face turns a person to
stone, so try sneaking up on her with your
back turned, using a mirror or another shiny
surface to keep an eye on her.

Beast Power

Strength	1
Repulsiveness	6
Special Powers	6
Ferocity	4
Invincibility	5

Total 22/50

Where does this myth come from?

In his long poem the Odyssey, *Homer described just one Gorgon who lived in Hades, the Underworld. Other Greek poets mentioned as many as three gorgons and Hesiod imagined them living in the sea, where they created reefs from the creatures they turned to stone.*

Elephant-Snake of the Jungle
Grootslang

The undergrowth crackled as the explorer pushed his way into the heart of the jungle. Here, the sun could not lighten the dark green gloom, and he did not see the creature coiled around the tree trunk ahead. Until . . .

. . . a weird trumpeting sound split the silence. He stopped. A giant beast stood before him. It had a massive elephant's head with two sets of tusks and a thick, serpentine body packed with muscle.

Turning to run, the explorer slipped. The creature slithered down toward him, its coils propelling it forward relentlessly . . .

How to defeat Grootslang

Perhaps a pair of poisoned darts, aimed at the eyes, would allow enough time for someone to escape Grootslang. Climbing trees is not an option, so it would be best to keep to the jungle floor, and cross water when possible so the beast loses your trail.

Where does this myth come from?

In some African folklore, the Grootslang was made by the gods in the mists of time. The gods then realized they'd made a mistake, which they later corrected by dividing each of these beasts into the elephant and the snake. But one Grootslang escaped and became the sire of all Grootslangs.

Beast Power

Strength
6

Repulsiveness
4

Special Powers
2

Ferocity
5

Invincibility
7

Total
24/50

Terror in the Labyrinth
The Minotaur

Part bull, part man, the Minotaur lived at the heart of an intricate underground maze on the island of Crete. Fourteen young men and maidens were regularly shipped from Athens as a living banquet for the beast.

At times, several of the young men tried to overpower the monster. But it gored them on its horns, while the others fled down the blind and baffling tunnels.

Then, bellowing with laughter, the Minotaur would track them down, for no one could find the way out. Soon he had eaten each young man and maiden whole . . .

—))•(•((—

How to defeat the Minotaur

The Greek hero Theseus finally killed the Minotaur in single combat. He found his way in and out of the labyrinth because Ariadne, daughter of the king of Crete, had given him a ball of thread to mark the route from the entrance.

Where does this myth come from?

One of the most famous monsters in Greek mythology, the Minotaur was described by poets and historians around the first century CE. The Roman poet Ovid also mentions him in his epic poem Metamorphoses as "a man half bull and a bull half man."

Beast Power

Strength
7

Repulsiveness
4

Special Powers
0

Ferocity
7

Invincibility
7

Total
25/50

The Dog of Hades
Cerberus

How gloomy was the land around the entrance to the Underworld! This was the domain of Cerberus, the giant, three-headed hound of Hades. His serpent tail waved in malevolent delight as he welcomed the spirits of the dead, licking their feet and herding them into the darkness of the Underworld.

How to defeat Cerberus

The hound was subdued by the heavenly music of Orpheus and the superhuman strength of Hercules, who had to capture Cerberus for his twelfth and most difficult Labor. The hero choked him into submission, but for a less powerful mortal, soothing music would work better.

Where does this myth come from?

Cerberus is famous in Greek mythology as the guardian of Hades, the Underworld, and assistant of its dark deity, also called Hades. He is mentioned by the Greek poet Homer simply as "the dog." The poet Hesiod called him Cerberus in the eighth century BCE.

Beast Power

Strength
8

Repulsiveness
5

Special Powers
0

Ferocity
9

Invincibility
9

Total
31/50

Gluttonous Whirlpool
Charybdis

A flotilla of boats sailed back and forth over the green-blue sea. Suddenly the sailors cried out in alarm and began rowing away at full speed . . . because very, very quietly, the surface of the water had lifted in a sweeping curve. For a moment, all was still, as in the eye of a storm. Then, with a deep roar, the water swirled downward, sucked by a force that tore the ocean wide open, right down to the dark seabed. The boats slipped helplessly into the vortex, as sailors were hurled overboard, shrieking.

How to defeat Charybdis

No one ever escaped the giant whirlpool. Ancient Greek heroes survived by avoiding it altogether.

Where does this myth come from?

The tale of Charybdis is a classic of Greek mythology and appears in the poem the Odyssey *by Homer. Around the first century BCE, Roman poets gave their own versions of the story.*

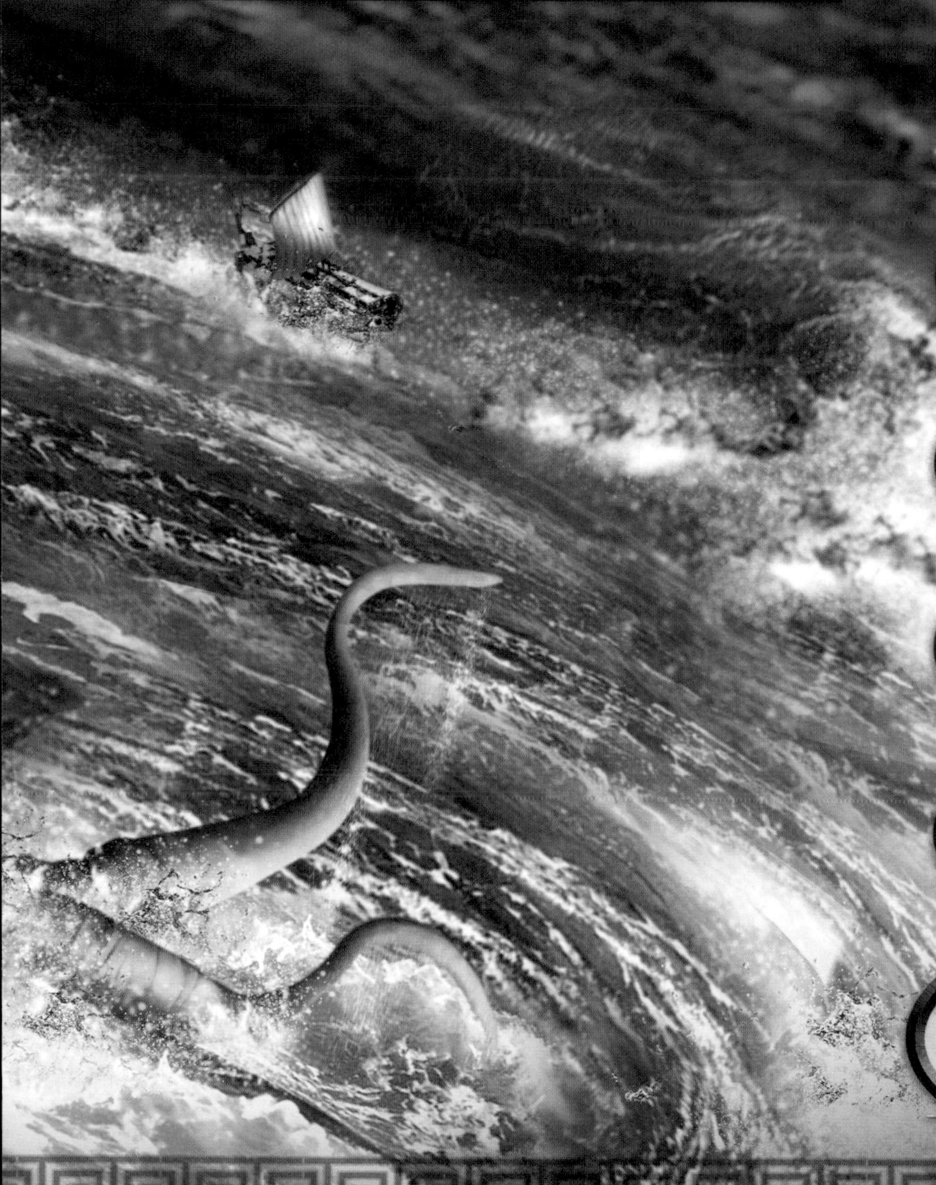

Beast Power

Strength
10

Repulsiveness
0

Special Powers
2

Ferocity
10

Invincibility
10

Total 32/50

Supreme Sea Demon
Scylla

Sailors who veered too far from the crazed whirlpool Charybdis faced another sea horror: Scylla. Hidden in a cave at the bottom of a cliff, this six-headed being leaped up and yelped like an excited puppy when a ship came near.

But she was no friendly puppy. Her six pairs of eyes burned with ravenous hunger, and her six jaws gaped open to show rows of hideously sharp teeth.

Acting in unison, the heads plunged into the ship as if it were a feeding trough and scooped up a man . . . or two. With a crunch and a gulp, each one disappeared, and Scylla began licking her jaws clean.

How to defeat Scylla

At least six people, all acting together, would be needed for this challenge. Perhaps they could fire flares down each gaping throat, so that Scylla would be distracted long enough for potential victims to make their escape.

Where does this myth come from?

Scylla occurs in many ancient sources along with her counterpart, Charybdis. In the Odyssey, *Homer gives her twelve feet and six long necks and mouths, calling her a plague on mankind. The Roman poet Ovid describes her as surrounded by dogs that devoured her prey.*

Beast Power

Strength
9

Repulsiveness
9

Special Powers
0

Ferocity
8

Invincibility
8

**Total
34/50**

Devourer of the Dead
Ammut

In the Hall of Two Truths, the jackal-headed god Anubis prepared to judge one more dead soul. Nearby stood snarling Ammut, guardian of the Scales of Justice.

The god placed the deceased person's heart on one side of the scales and the Feather of Truth on the other. Only a heart that was lighter than the feather would allow the person a happy afterlife. Otherwise, it would be devoured by the snarling Ammut.

How to defeat Ammut

Be a very, very good person so that your heart will pass the test. Or place a fake, lightweight heart in the Scales, or slip something heavy under the feather . . .

Beast Power

Strength
9

Repulsiveness
6

Special Powers
1

Ferocity
10

Invincibility
10

Total
36/50

Where does this myth come from?

Ammut features in the ancient Egyptian Book of the Dead. *This is a collection of texts, some written on papyrus, some on tomb walls. The texts were spells to help the dead travel safely through the Underworld. One of the best-preserved copies dates from 1240 BCE.*

Nine-Headed Serpent
The Hydra

Its lair was a cave by the swampy lake of Lerna. Nine heads grew from its snake body, and its breath poisoned the air, so that anyone passing close by might simply choke to death. Its blood, too, was poisonous, and if it lost one of its heads, two more grew in its place.

Now Hercules faced the Hydra as his second Labor. He fired arrows into its cave to bring the infuriated creature slithering out, its long necks writhing and heads snapping.

Hercules darted here and there, out of reach of the crushing fangs, and with a lightning blow severed one of the heads. But how could he stop new ones from growing?

How to defeat the Hydra

Even mighty Hercules needed help to do this. As he cut off each of the Hydra's heads, his nephew Iolaus cauterized the blood vessels with burning torches to stop another two heads from growing.

Where does this myth come from?

The Hydra and its battle with Hercules are often detailed by the Greek and Roman poets starting in the eighth century BCE. Greek geographers even used the myth when they described an area called Argolis in southern Greece, the location of Lake Lerna.

Beast
Power

Strength
9

Repulsiveness
9

Special Powers
8

Ferocity
8

Invincibility
8

Total
42/50

Rogues' Gallery

10
The Harpies
The "snatchers" or "hounds of Zeus," as they were known, were pursued by the two winged Argonauts as far as the Strophades, islands in western Greece.

9
Gugalanna
Flocks of sheep fled from their pens in terror from this rampaging bull. After Gilgamesh had slain Gugalanna, he fed the bull's meat to his starving people.

6
The Minotaur
He was the offspring of Queen Pasiphaë of Crete and a bull sent as a gift to King Minos by Poseidon. The maze was built by Minos's brilliant architect, Daedalus.

5
Cerberus
Hercules dragged the hound, barking frantically, up to Earth. Along the way, the poisonous aconite plant sprang up where drops of the creature's saliva fell.

2
Ammut
Part crocodile, part lion, and part hippopotamus, Ammut was associated with Amenta, the west bank of the Nile where Egyptian cemeteries were located. Amenta was also the name of the Underworld, and one ancient picture shows Ammut crouching by its infernal fires.

8

The Gorgons

Even the sight of an urn containing some of of Medusa's snake-hair was enough to cause an entire army to flee.

7

Grootslang

Its name means "big snake." It it was thought to dwell in a diamond-filled cave and to be the cause of human disappearances.

4

Charybdis

To avoid the dreaded whirlpool, the Greek hero Odysseus sailed close to nearby Scylla instead. This meant he might lose six men, rather than his entire crew.

3

Scylla

Homer describes how Scylla threw Odysseus's men onto the nearby rocks and then began devouring them one by one, as they called for their captain.

1

The Hydra

The Hydra's central head was immortal, so Hercules attacked it last of all, cutting it off at the neck. He buried it underground with a boulder on top, then chopped up her body and cast the pieces into the swamp. He dipped his arrows in the Hydra's spilled blood. When used against humans or gods, they caused wounds that were agonizing and incurable.

Want to Know More?

Hera's Pet

The Hydra was the offspring of the monster Typhon and a half-snake, half-woman, Echidna. She was brought up by the great goddess Hera, who turned her into an almost invincible fiend in the hope that she would destroy Hercules. Hera had an undying hatred of Hercules, because he was the son of her husband Zeus and a mortal, Alcmena.

Once fully grown, the Hydra went to live by a lake in eastern Greece where the waters were known for their purity—but not after the monster had spread her smelly fumes around. She also terrorized the local people, who would have been very, very glad of help from Hercules.

When Hera observed her prodigy in battle with the hero, she sent a giant crab to help the Hydra. The crab came scuttling out of the swamp and pinched Hercules' foot, but he easily crushed the crustacean. After the battle, Hera, who liked to immortalize her creatures, turned the Hydra into a constellation (the largest in the sky) and the crab into the neighboring constellation of Cancer.

Gorgon News

Of the three Gorgons, who were the children of the sea deities Phorcys and Ceto, only Medusa was mortal. One of the most famous of the Greek myths is the tale of her decapitation by the hero Perseus . . . for which he needed much help from the gods. They gave him a sword, a helmet that made him invisible, winged sandals, and a shiny shield in which he could safely look at Medusa's reflection.

After Perseus had cut off her head, the winged horse Pegasus was born from Medusa's blood. Now Perseus had his own magical flying steed . And that was not the end of the Medusa impact. With Medusa's head in a bag, Perseus flew over North Africa, where Atlas held up the sky. When Atlas threatened him, Perseus showed him the Gorgon's head, and Atlas became a petrified mountain range.

At the Red Sea, corals were formed from Medusa's blood oozing into the waters, while drops spilled over the Sahara created a swarm of vipers. In a final flourish, Perseus saved his mother from a forced marriage to King Polydectes by turning the husband-to-be to stone. A Medusa head can be a very useful traveling companion!

Stories in Stone

The Gilgamesh story was inscribed on clay in a wedge-shaped script called cuneiform. This makes it a very early example of writing as well as storytelling.

Another text tells how, when Gilgamesh died, he was buried under the Euphrates River. In 2003 a team of German archaeologists working in the Iraqi desert claimed to have found the entire city of Uruk, which Gilgamesh ruled. Nearby they uncovered the possible remains of the king's tomb in the former riverbed. They also found structures, such as gardens and a system of canals, just like those described in the *Epic of Gilgamesh*.

Index

The Author

Alice Peebles is an editor and writer specializing in the arts and humanities for children. She is a coauthor of *Encyclopedia of Art for Young People* and one of the creators of *The Guzunder Gang* audiobook series. She has also edited and written for several children's magazines focused on history, art, geography. She lives in London, England.

The Artist

Nigel Chilvers is a digital illustrator based in the United Kingdom. He has illustrated numerous children's books.